Weekend Fun

Let's Go to the
Beach

By Mary Hill

Children's Press®
A Division of Scholastic Inc.
New York / Toronto / London / Auckland / Sydney
Mexico City / New Delhi / Hong Kong
Danbury, Connecticut

Photo Credits: Cover © Corbis; all other images by Maura B. McConnell
Contributing Editors: Shira Laskin and Jennifer Silate
Book Design: Michael DeLisio

Library of Congress Cataloging-in-Publication Data

Hill, Mary, 1977-
    Let's go to the beach / by Mary Hill.
    p. cm.—(Weekend fun)
    Summary: A young girl describes some of the activities she and her
    family enjoy during a day at the beach.
    ISBN 0-516-23994-5 (lib. bdg.)—ISBN 0-516-25921-0 (pbk.)
    1. Beaches—Recreational use—Juvenile literature. 2. Outdoor
    recreation—Juvenile literature. 3. Seashore—Juvenile literature. [1.
    Beaches.] I. Title. II. Series.

    GV191.62.H55 2003
    796.5'3—dc21

                                                    2003010818

Contents

My name is Sadie.

My parents and I are going to the beach today.

Mom and Dad put our **blanket** on the sand.

I wear a **bathing suit** at the beach.

I cannot wait to go into the water!

9

Mom puts **sunscreen** on my skin.

This will keep my skin safe from the Sun.

We play in the ocean.

I jump over **waves**.

13

We go back to our blanket when we are finished playing in the water.

We will eat **sandwiches** for lunch.

We walk along the beach to look for shells after lunch.

I bring a **pail** to hold the shells I find.

17

Dad and I build a **sandcastle**.

I put a shell on it.

It is time to go home.

We had fun at the beach today!

WELCOME TO OCEAN CI

• THIS OCEAN IS ALWAYS DANGEROUS.
  BATHE AT GUARDED BEACHES ONLY.

• DESIGNATED BEACHE ARE GUARDED
  DAY THROUGH LABOR DAY. AFTER LA
  CALL FOR A LISTING OF GUARDED B8
  WEEKDAYS: 10:00AM
  WEEKENDS & HOLIDAYS: 10:00AM

• FOR UPDATED INFORMATION ON GUAR
  BEACHES:
        DIAL 609-814-WAVE (9)
        RADIO 1620 AM
        TV CHANNEL 2

• PLEASE FOLLOW ALL LIFEGUARDS INS

• FOR YOUR SAFETY, SWIM OR BATHE
  DESIGNATED AREA AND ONLY WHEN
  ARE ON DUTY.

• THE AREA BETWEEN GREEN FLA
  DESIGNATED AREA WHERE LIFEGUARD
  DUTY.

FOR ALL EMERGENCIES DIAL

21

New Words

bathing suit (**bayth**-ing **soot**) a piece of clothing that people wear to go swimming

blanket (**blang**-kit) a large piece of cloth that fits on a bed

pail (**payl**) a round container with a handle and a flat bottom used for water, sand, or other things

sandcastle (**sand**-cas-uhl) a castle that is made out of sand

sandwiches (**sand**-wich-iss) food made with two pieces of bread and meat, cheese, peanut butter, or some other food between them

sunscreen (**suhn**-skreen) a cream or lotion that keeps the skin safe from the Sun

waves (**wayvz**) moving ridges on the surface of water, especially the ocean

To Find Out More

Books

Did You Ever Wonder about Things You Find at the Beach?
by Vera Vullo Capogna
Marshall Cavendish Corp.

Going to the Beach
by Jo S. Kittinger
Scholastic Library Publishing

Web Site
Beach Kids Zone
http://www.learnenglish.org.uk/kids/archive/theme_beach.html
Learn about the beach, read jokes, and play games on this Web site.

Index

About the Author

Mary Hill has written many books for children. For fun on the weekends, she likes to go sailing.

Reading Consultants

Kris Flynn, Coordinator, Small School District Literacy, The San Diego County Office of Education

Shelly Forys, Certified Reading Recovery Specialist, W.J. Zahnow Elementary School, Waterloo, IL

Paulette Mansell, Certified Reading Recovery Specialist, and Early Literacy Consultant, TX